RENEW

A Basic Guide for a

PERSONAL RETREAT

by David Sherbino

Renew

A BASIC GUIDE FOR A PERSONAL RETREAT

DR. DAVID SHERBINO

CASTLE QUAY BOOKS

WWW.CASTLEQUAYBOOKS.COM

RENEW: A BASIC GUIDE FOR A PERSONAL RETREAT

Copyright © 2015 David Sherbino
All rights reserved
Printed in Canada
International Standard Book Number: 978-1-927355-72-5
ISBN 978-1-927355-73-2 EPUB

Published by:
Castle Quay Books
19-24 Laguna Pkwy, Lagoon City, Brechin, Ontario, L0K 1B0
Tel: (416) 573-3249
E-mail: info@castlequaybooks.com   www.castlequaybooks.com

Edited by Marina Hofman Willard
Cover design by Burst Impressions
Printed at Essence Printing, Belleville, Ontario

Library and Archives Canada Cataloguing in Publication

Sherbino, David, author
      Renew : a basic guide for a personal retreat / David Sherbino.

ISBN 978-1-927355-72-5 (paperback)

      1. Spiritual retreats. 2. Spiritual exercises. 3. Spiritual life--Christianity. I. Title.

BV5068.R4S55 2015   269'.6   C2015-905914-3

CASTLE QUAY BOOKS
www.castlequaybooks.com

TABLE
of
CONTENTS

Part I: Renewed Through Retreat

Part II: Practices for Your Retreat

"You, God, are my God,
earnestly I seek you;
I thirst for you,
my whole being longs for you,
in a dry and parched land
where there is no water."

Psalm 63:1

PART I

RENEWED
Through
RETREAT

"A good journey begins knowing where we are and being willing to go somewhere else."

—Richard Rohr[1]

Section 1

The
NEED
for a
RETREAT

Life is busy with lots of demands, and many would acknowledge that they are overextended, exhausted and stressed out. In fact, some would say they don't even have time to catch their breath. In the Gospels, there are different accounts of Jesus and the disciples deliberately leaving behind the demands of life and retreating to a quiet place in order to be renewed. This reinforces the concept that a retreat is a necessity for each one of us in today's world.

The popular concept of a retreat today is somewhat different than the one used by Jesus. For example, if you are engaged in youth ministry, the term "retreat" brings to mind the task of organizing endless activities to keep the youth occupied, to the extent that most leaders and participants return home exhausted. A retreat for adult members of a church congregation usually includes Bible study, teaching and extended periods of corporate worship. In some instances a retreat is viewed as an opportunity to work together with a particular group on some project related to its faith community.

Throughout his life and ministry Jesus would regularly retreat to a quiet place for extended periods of time just to be alone with the Father. Before he began his ministry, we are told, he was led by the Spirit into the wilderness, where he fasted and prayed for 40 days (Matthew 4:1–11). Mark gives us a glimpse into the demands of just one day of Jesus' ministry. He went to Capernaum, where he taught in the synagogue, cast out evil spirits, healed Simon's mother-in-law from a fever, and then in the evening, when the sick and demon-possessed came to the home of Simon Peter, he healed them as well. It was a busy day, to say the least. The next morning the disciples were looking for Jesus, but Jesus could not be found. He had risen early that morning to go to a lonely place, where he prayed (Mark 1:1–39). As you read through the Gospels you will discover that retreating to places of silence and solitude was a regular practice for Jesus (Matthew 14:23; Matthew 21:17; Luke 22:39–46).

Not only did Jesus practice this discipline, it was also a practice that he wanted his disciples to embrace in their ministry. When Jesus commissioned the disciples, he told them to preach the message "The kingdom of heaven is near." And they were to heal the sick, raise the dead and cast out demons (Matthew 10:7–8). They faced a challenging ministry, to say the least. When they went out to minister, they saw God transforming the lives of people as they preached the gospel, healed the sick and cast out demons (Mark 6:12–13). When they returned from their assignment, they reported everything they had experienced to Jesus. In fact, they were so excited that they wanted to go out immediately and continue the ministry, but Jesus told them, "Come with me by yourselves to a quiet place and get some rest" (Mark 6:31). In essence Jesus was telling them to "come away and be renewed." In other words, allow God to do in you what he will ultimately do through you.

Sadly, there are many who feel their lives are unravelling, and they are exhausted and stressed out. As the demands of life and ministry increase, some try to work longer and harder to accomplish the tasks that are before them. Many of these tasks may be good and legitimate, but the price many pay is that their inner life withers because it is neglected.

Take a few minutes to think about what might happen if you took an extended period of time—perhaps one or two days—away from your normal routine in the next month just to be alone with God. What do you think would happen? I am sure most would come up with many positive answers, such as "I would be less stressed out" or "I would be able to have a greater sense of peace in my life" or "I would be able to think more creatively" or "I would be able to hear the voice of God more clearly."

In spite of all the good reasons we can think of, we can also come up with just as many good excuses not to take time to be away. "I am too busy" or "I don't think I can be alone and quiet by myself" or "I will do it later, when my life settles down."

You will need to decide what you will do. You can listen to the voice of your excuses, or you can listen to the voice of God. The purpose of a retreat is to enable you to be free from outside distractions so you can hear what God wants to say to you. If you find that your life is being pulled in many different directions, it can be a time to refocus and get a new sense of direction and purpose. For others, time alone will enable them to experience God more intimately by simply being in his presence. For everyone, it will be an opportunity to rest and to be renewed. The Old Testament prophet Elijah confronted the prophets of Baal and won a decisive victory over them.

However, he was exhausted from the encounter and fled to the wilderness. It was during his time in the wilderness that God provided for all of his needs and enabled him to continue the journey (1 Kings 18–20).

---

[1] Richard Rohr, quoted in Ruth Haley Barton, *Invitation to Solitude and Silence: Experiencing God's Transforming Presence* (Downers Grove: IVP 2004), 25.

"The deepest desire of our hearts is for union with God.
From the first moment of our existence,
our most powerful yearning is to fulfill the
original purpose of our lives—to see Him more clearly,
to love Him more dearly, to follow Him more nearly,
as the old prayer says. We are made for God,
and nothing less will really satisfy us."

—Brennan Manning[1]

Section 2

The PURPOSE of a RETREAT

As you consider taking a retreat, keep in mind that the emphasis of the retreat is to help you develop and build your relationship with God. Ben Johnson and Paul Lang suggest that there are several reasons for taking a retreat.[2]

1. **A retreat will help you to attain balance in your life.**

    For those who are high achievers, it may be possible that in the quest for success everything else is sacrificed. Is the success sought worth the price being paid? On the other hand, there are those who lack purpose and direction in life. For them a retreat offers the opportunity to look deeply into their souls and determine what changes need to be made.

2. **A retreat offers the opportunity to focus on persistent questions of your life.**

    You can take the time to ask "What is the meaning of my life?" If we simply live each day without looking at the end goal of life, we can easily miss out on the purpose of life.

15

3. **A retreat offers the opportunity to examine personal relationships.**

   Do you take time to look at the relationships that are at the centre of your life? This can include family, friends, co-workers, neighbours and those in your community of faith. Are there issues that need to be resolved? Are there people you need to connect with more intentionally? Are there some relationships that you need to let go of because they are toxic or destructive?

4. **A retreat helps you to build into your life the rhythm of engagement and withdrawal.**

   Rhythm is built into the fabric of life. There is a rhythm to the seasons, there is a 24-hour rhythm that includes night and day, and God established a rhythm at creation when he declared six days of work and a seventh day of rest. As we examine our lives we can discern if we have a proper balance between engagement and withdrawal. Without this, we become consumed by a life of engagement that can easily overwhelm us.

5. **A retreat allows us the opportunity to establish or re-establish our relationship with God in new and different ways.**

   The great commandment of Scripture is "You shall love the Lord your God with all your heart and with all your soul and with all your mind…And a second is like it: You shall love your neighbor as yourself" (Matthew 22:37–39 ESV). Do you truly love God, and is this love being expressed in your relationship with others? Time alone will allow you to explore these and other questions.

Do any or all of these reasons convince you of the need to take some time away to be alone with God?

[1] Brennan Manning, *Abba's Child: The Cry of the Heart for Intimate Belonging* (Colorado Springs: Tyndale House Publishers, 1994, 2002, 2015), 24.

[2] Ben Campbell Johnson and Paul H. Lang, *Time Away* (Nashville: Upper Room Books, 2010), 24–28.

Section 3

ORGANIZING
and
PREPARING
for a
RETREAT

Some will consider taking a one-day retreat, while others might consider a longer period of two or three days. If this is the first time you have taken a personal retreat, you may be wondering what you are going to do. This guide will offer a few suggestions.

Recognize that these are simply guidelines and that the focus is to be able to interact with God. To do this you will need to be rested and refreshed, so do not feel compelled to do all the reflection exercises. If you are tired, take a nap; if you need to have a change of scenery, take a walk or go for a swim. You choose what is best for you.

The main reason for the retreat is to create an openness to God and to listen to what he has to say to you. With that in mind, there are a few things to consider as you plan this time.

1. Do not bring a list of things you need to accomplish, such as books to read or emails to write. This is not a time to work; think of this as time alone with God. Therefore consider

why you are going on this retreat and what you hope to receive from God.

2. Try not to arrive exhausted. If you are too tired, you will want to sleep most of the time. This in and of itself may be an indicator that you need to consider bringing more balance into your life.

3. Plan to turn off all electronic devices while on retreat. If people want to connect with you, make sure it is an emergency. Give them the phone number of the retreat centre, and the personnel at the retreat centre can relay the necessary information to you.

4. Be sure to bring a Bible, notebook and journal. This will help you stay focused as you record your thoughts and ideas. I am a bit skeptical about using electronic devices to record your thoughts. The temptation to retrieve emails or surf the net can be difficult to resist.

5. If there are activities you enjoy such as hiking, swimming, photography, painting, sketching, etc., remember to bring the essential clothing and equipment.

6. Consider bringing a songbook or hymnal.

7. Bring your day planner. There will be an opportunity to reflect on your past activities and offer future plans to God as you seek to develop a balanced rhythm of life.

Section 4

CHOOSING
a
RETREAT
CENTRE

Choose a retreat centre that will accommodate your needs. Do you want to prepare your own meals or have them prepared? Do you wish to eat alone or in the company of others? What types of activities do you want to participate in (hiking, swimming)? Do you want to participate in community worship at the retreat centre? Do you want to meet with a spiritual director? Find out about the scheduled activities during your time on retreat. If you are seeking a place for silence and solitude, a retreat centre that focuses on highly interactive events will not be suitable for your needs.

For local retreat centres, Google "retreat centres" and your area. You will likely find a suitable place that is conveniently located near you. Here is a list of retreat centres within driving distance of the Greater Toronto Area:

1. **Canterbury Hills** —Ancaster, ON; 1 (800) 463–3193; www.canterburyhills.ca

2. **Crieff Hills Community**—Puslinch, ON; 1 (519) 824–7898; www.crieffhills.com

3. **Eramosa Eden** —Rockwood, ON; 1 (519) 856–4209; www.eramosaeden.org

4. **Five Oaks**—Paris, ON; 1 (519) 856 4209; www.fiveoaks.on.ca

5. **Home of Bethany** —Sunderland, ON; 1 (705) 357–3972; www.canadianbest.com/Home-of-Bethany/

6. **Loyola House** —Guelph, ON; 1 (519) 824–1250; www.loyolahouse.ca

7. **Manresa Renewal Centre** —Pickering, ON; 1 (905) 893–2864; www.manresa-canada.ca

8. **Mount Alverno Retreat Centre** —Caledon, ON; 1 (519) 941–7059; www.mountalverno.ca

9. **Queen of Apostles** —Mississauga, ON; 1 (905) 278–5229; www.qoa.ca

10. **The Sisterhood of St. John the Divine** —North York, ON; 1 (416) 226–2201; www.ssjd.ca

11. **St. Francis Centre** —Orangeville, ON; 1 (519) 941–1747; http://stfranciscentre.org/

12. **3 Crosses** —Huntsville, ON; 1 (705) 349–8655; www.3crosses.ning.com

"Solitude eventually offers a quiet gift of grace,
a gift that comes whenever we are able to face
ourselves honestly: the gift of acceptance,
of compassion, for who we are as we are.
As we allow ourselves to be known in solitude,
we discover that we are known by love.
Beyond the pain of self-discovery there is a love
that does not condemn us but calls us to itself.
This love receives us as we are."

—Parker Palmer[1]

Section 5

The
STRUCTURE
of a
RETREAT

There is no set structure for a retreat; therefore you need to find a rhythm that best suits you. The first thing to remember about a retreat is that you start to slow things down. There is no need to be in a rush; the retreat will afford you the opportunity to take in the sights, sounds, colours and silence around you. You may also choose to do something creative, such as paint a picture, take some photographs or go for a walk in nature and discover some of the beauty of creation.

Take periods of time to rest. You are not living by the clock, and there are no tasks to accomplish, so if you are tired, take a nap. For others, rest may include some physical activity, such as hiking, swimming, bicycle riding or just sitting outside in the evening and looking at the sky.

Learn to appreciate silence. This is a critical aspect of a personal retreat. Many people are activists and are accustomed to a lot of activity and commotion in life. If we are going to hear God speak, we must learn to be silent. The psalmist wrote, "Be still,

25

and know that I am God" (Psalm 46:10). Let's be honest—this will be a challenge, but once you begin to enter into silence you will discover how powerful it is.

Choose an environment that is inviting and free of distractions. Some will try to have a retreat in their home, but for most this is a distracting environment; the phone may ring, you will see chores that need to be done, or people may drop in unannounced. In choosing a retreat centre you are intentionally getting away from everything that reminds you of your normal daily routine.

---

[1] Parker Palmer, quoted in Haley Barton, *Invitation to Solitude and Silence*, 108.

*"Give thanks in all circumstances,
for this is God's will for you in Christ Jesus."*

1 Thessalonians 5:18

*"To be grateful is to recognize the Love of God
in everything He has given us—
and He has given us everything...
Gratitude therefore takes nothing for granted,
is never unresponsive, is constantly awakening to
new wonder and to praise of the goodness of God.
For the grateful person knows that God is good,
not by hearsay but by experience.
And that is what makes the difference."*

—Thomas Merton[1]

Section 6

SAMPLE STRUCTURE *of a* ONE-DAY RETREAT

This is a very simple guide. There are several suggestions on how to structure your day, including set times. However, remember, this is only a guide, and you need to be free to organize your day according to your needs. The example structures here utilize the practices described in later sections. You may want to read through the practices to become familiar with different approaches to Scripture reading and prayer exercises.

MORNING SESSION

8:30 a.m.

- Arrive at the retreat centre. Have breakfast before you leave home.

- Get settled into your environment. Take some time to be quiet and allow your body to relax.

8:45 a.m.

- Begin the retreat by offering your day unto God and giving over to him all you are leaving behind. This may include worries, business issues, family struggles or some other challenges.

- Praise. Turn your thoughts toward God and enter into the worship of him. Slowly read a psalm and let the words speak into your life. You might write down any thoughts that seem to resonate with you and pray these thoughts back to God. Some suggested psalms are 9, 19, 24, 33, 34, 46, 81, 84, 96, 98,145, 149 and 150.

- If you have a hymnal or songbook, sing a song of praise or offer a prayer of praise unto the Lord.

10:00 a.m.

- Break. Take a short break, go for a silent walk, enjoy a cup of coffee or simply gaze out the window.

10:15 a.m.

- Thanksgiving. Begin this segment with thanksgiving. Read Psalm 136:1–9, 23–26. As you read this psalm think about your own life and how you can begin to thank God for
    - his goodness
    - his creation
    - his saving grace
    - his daily provision
    - his enduring love
- You may find it helpful to write the prayer in your journal.
- Write out the names of people you are thankful for and offer a prayer of thanksgiving, mentioning each one by name and why you are thankful for each one.

11:15 a.m.

- Take a short break.

11:30 a.m.

- Confession. The final part of the morning can be focused on prayers of confession and examination of conscience. There are times when we need to examine our relationship with God and with others. We all hurt and wound each other, at times intentionally and at other times unintentionally. Allow God to speak into your life. Begin this prayer session by asking God to reveal to you areas of your life that need to be confessed. Sit quietly and write down in your journal whatever God brings to your remembrance. Allow the Holy Spirit to bring to your awareness the areas of your life that need to be confessed. At times it can be helpful if you have kept a journal to read your entries over the past period of time. The Holy Spirit will use this to prompt your recall. As you write down areas of your life that need to be confessed, pray through each item and confess it to God. At the conclusion of this prayer, be assured of God's forgiveness. It can be helpful to read passages such as

  Therefore encourage one another and build one another up. (1 Thessalonians 5:11 ESV)

  For as high as the heavens are above the earth, So great is His lovingkindness toward those who fear Him. As far as the east is from the west, So far has He removed our transgressions from us. (Psalm 103:11–12 NASB)

- Another method of praying prayers of confession is to read a psalm such as 32 or 51 and base your prayer on themes found in the text.

- Other people find it helpful to use the practice of the prayer of examen. (See Part II, Section 1.)

12:30 p.m.

- Lunch. Enjoy the gifts of food and drink that God provides. Do not hurry through lunch; take time to savour the food. After lunch you might want to take a walk or perhaps enjoy a nap. If necessary, give yourself permission to do so. Remember, God desires that we care for the body. If you are tired, it is an indicator that you need to rest. Enjoy!

AFTERNOON SESSION

1:30 p.m.

- Pray for others. A retreat is a wonderful time to spend in extended unhurried prayer for other people. Who are the people in your life that you are committed to pray for? It may include your immediate family, friends, co-workers and members of your faith community, or you might be drawn to pray for people you do not know but whose situation you are aware of through the media, such as the poor and the marginalized. Since every person's situation is different, your prayers may focus on thanksgiving, petition or confession, depending on the person you are praying for at this time.

- Instead of praying a prayer that focuses on "God bless…" use Scripture as a template to pray for people. The apostle Paul has written four prayers you might use as a guide. (See Part II, Section 2.)

2:30 p.m.

- Break. Take some time to go for a walk or enjoy a light snack and reflect on what God has impressed upon you during this prayer session.

3:00 p.m.

- Pray for self. Having prayed for others, now think about your own life. Bring your plans and hopes and dreams before God. Again, the focus is not so much on what you are trying to accomplish; rather, pray that your life will be pleasing to God.

- You may be in a season of life when you need wisdom and discernment about choices you are making. Perhaps you need to explore some of the ups and downs or struggles you are facing in life or attitudes that may be blocking your openness to God. These issues could be the focus of your prayer. Remember, God is interested in every facet of life because all life belongs to him.

4:00 p.m.

- Prepare to go home. Take a few minutes to review the day. What have you discovered? What are the changes you wish to make? Offer this to God, and give thanks as you return home.

---

[1] Thomas Merton, *Thoughts in Solitude* (New York: Farrar, Straus and Giroux, 1999), 33.

"I am clean for I have confessed.
I shall be clean till I sin...
Then I shall confess
and be clean again.
Confession is the window of grace.
We confess and the sunlight
of wholeness streams in through
the streaked glass of our compromises,
cleansing as it comes."

—Calvin Miller[1]

Section 7

SAMPLE STRUCTURE *of a* THREE-DAY RETREAT

If it is possible, arrive at the retreat centre in the afternoon or evening to begin your retreat. This will enable you to get settled and rested as you begin your retreat. The outline for each day is only a suggestion, and you may wish to change it to suit your needs. Plan to be silent as much as is possible.

THE FIRST EVENING

6:00 p.m.

- Get settled. Check out your environment and become familiar with the various places at the retreat centre, such as the dining room, the chapel, recreation facilities, hiking paths.

7:00 p.m.

- Enjoy a leisurely dinner.

- Take a relaxing walk before settling in for the night.
- Conclude your evening with devotional reading and evening prayer.

DAY ONE

7:30 a.m.

- Rise and prepare for the day.

8:00 a.m.

- Engage in morning prayer. Read a psalm and work through the practice of praying the psalms. (See Part II, Section 3.) Sit in silence before God. Offer the day to the Lord, giving thanks for the rest of the evening and committing to him the day as it unfolds. If the retreat centre has community morning prayer, you may choose to join in the prayer.

8:30 a.m.

- Breakfast.

9:30 a.m.

- Exercise holy reading. Read a biblical passage using the practice of holy reading. (See Part II, Section 4.)

10:30 a.m.

- Take a break, enjoy a cup of coffee or go for a walk.

11:00 a.m.

- Review your life. Take some time to think about your life and important markers in your journey as well as people who have been a major influence in your life.
  - Childhood, 1–12
  - Adolescence, 13–17
  - Young adulthood, 18–35
  - Midlife, 35–65
  - Senior, 65+
- What are the insights you have gained about your life?
- How can you offer this to God?

12:30 p.m.

- Lunch. Mealtimes are an opportunity to rest, to reflect and to enjoy the gift of food that God has provided. All too often we rush through our meals so that we can move on to the next task. This is a time to express gratitude to God for the gift of the fruit of the earth, which we can easily take for granted.

1:30 p.m.

- Rest.

2:30 p.m.

- Silence and solitude. Use this period of silent reflection to be quiet and to listen to God. You may want to be outside. Try to listen to God through creation as well as to listen to him speak through your thoughts where you hear the whisper of God's voice. If this is a first time for you to be silent for more than a few minutes, do not be surprised at the noise in your head. You will likely feel distracted, since there are so many voices calling for your attention. Simply write them down and offer them to God. Try to discover what he is telling you through this experience.

6:00 p.m.

• Supper.

7:00 p.m.

• The prayer of examen. Take some time to journal your thoughts and what you have discovered during the day. At the end of the day, pray through the practice of the prayer of examen. (See Part II, Section 1.)

DAY TWO

7:30 a.m.

• Rise and prepare for the day.

8:00 a.m.

• Engage in morning prayer. Meditate on the same psalm as yesterday, or read a different psalm. Sit in silence before God. Offer the day to the Lord, giving thanks for the first day of the retreat and the ways God spoke to you. Commit the day to listening to the Holy Spirit again. If the retreat centre has community morning prayer, you may choose to join in the prayer.

8:30 a.m.

• Breakfast.

9:30 a.m.

- Practice Gospel contemplation. This is an opportunity for you to hear what Christ would say to you today. (See Part II, Section 5.)

11:30 a.m.

- Break. Consider going for a walk or participating in a nature activity.

12:30 p.m.

- Lunch.

1:30 p.m.

- Rest.

2:30 p.m.

- Reflection. Take this time to do some soul-searching. Consider the questions in the appendix. (See Part II, Section 6.)

4:00 p.m.

- Take a break; enjoy a hot or cold drink.

4:30 p.m.

- Listen to creation. Read Psalm 8 slowly and meditatively, and then with paper and pen in hand simply sit and look at a creation. Write down any discoveries or reflections that come to you.

6:00 p.m.

- Dinner.

7:00 p.m.

- Pray with Scripture. Spend an hour in prayer using one of the Four Scripture Prayers. (See Part II, Section 2.) You may focus on praying for people who are part of your life, or perhaps you will use these prayers to focus on you own life. At the conclusion of this exercise, journal your reflections.

9:00 p.m.

- Conclude the day using the prayer of examen.

DAY 3

7:30 a.m.

- Rise and prepare for the day.

8:00 a.m.

- Engage in morning prayer. Read another psalm. Spend some time sitting in silence before God. Offer the day to the Lord again, with thanksgiving for this retreat and all the Holy Spirit has revealed. Commit the day to being attuned to the Holy Spirit. If the retreat centre has community morning prayer, you may choose to join in the prayer.

8:30 a.m.

- Breakfast.

9:30 a.m.

- Holy reading. (See Part II, Section 4.) Engage in the four steps of holy reading: reading and listening, meditation, prayer and contemplation.

10:30 a.m.

- Break.

11:00 a.m.

- Reflect on your personal rule of life. Take some time to review your day planner. Look at past activities, and then look at what you have scheduled to take place in the near future. Is there balance between work and rest? Do you have enough time for significant relationships? If you were to offer your schedule to God, would he be pleased? If not, what needs to be changed? Consider developing a rule of life. (See Part II, Section 7.)

12:30 p.m.

- Lunch.

1:30 p.m.

- Prepare to return home. Take some time to reflect on your retreat experience and what God has spoken into your life. What changes will you make? Will you commit to finding time on a regular daily or weekly basis to be alone with God? Write into your schedule your next extended retreat event. If you do not plan for the next retreat, it will not happen.

2:30 p.m.

- Leave for home.

---

[1] Calvin Miller, *Into the Depths of God* (Minneapolis: Bethany House Publishers, 2000), 190.

PART II

PRACTICES

for Your

RETREAT

The following section consists of a series of personal spiritual practices that have been used by the Church for centuries. These practices enable you to look closely at your life and explore issues that God may be impressing on your mind. An explanation of each of the practices will help you understand how to use these practices in a creative manner that will help you to grow in your relationship with God, others and self.

"Examination of the world without is never as personally painful as examination of the world within...Yet when one is dedicated to the truth this pain seems relatively unimportant."

—M. Scott Peck[1]

Section 1

The PRAYER of EXAMEN

The prayer of examen is a method of examining or reflecting upon one's life in such a manner that you will notice your days. In the process you discover how to love and serve God more fully. This prayer covers a very limited period of time; most often it is a recollection and reflection on the events of the past 24 hours.

Developed years ago by St. Ignatius, the prayer of examen has become a form of prayer that helps people enter into the presence of God in a more experiential manner and discover the different ways God reveals himself in daily life. St. Ignatius encouraged people to become aware of and to explore their deepest feelings and desires. Those feelings that help connect us with God, he referred to as "consolations," and those feelings that disconnect us with God, he referred to as "desolations." Thus, as I reflect upon my day, am I aware of having drawn closer to God, or am I aware of having moved away from God? Ignatius believed God would speak through these feelings and desires, but first we must become aware of what we are experiencing and seek to understand what is happening.

The prayer of examen is very flexible and simple to use as part of a daily routine. There are some who set aside two brief periods a day to pray this prayer, but most find it helpful to set aside five to ten minutes before going to bed to reflect on their day.

As you begin this prayer, it is important to take some time to become quiet and focused. Find a place where you will not be disturbed; sit comfortably and become relaxed. There are five steps to the prayer of examen, and they can easily be followed.

STEP ONE: RECALL THE PRESENCE OF GOD

"In him we live and move and have our being." (Acts 17:28 ESV)

Every day is filled with a variety of events and experiences. Some days are relaxed, while others are filled with tension. Some days are productive, while others are challenging. In the centre of all this activity, God is present. It is important to learn to slow down and reflect upon God's presence.

We understand theologically that God is always present, but in prayer we place ourselves in his presence in an attentive manner. God the Father loves and cares for you in the deepest possible way. Through Jesus Christ you know of your significance and value to God, and the Holy Spirit leads you into all truth so that you may know God more fully. So in this prayer begin by asking God to reveal himself to you.

STEP TWO: ASK THE HOLY SPIRIT TO HELP YOU

"When the Spirit of truth comes, he will guide you into all truth." (John 16:13 NLT)

Ask the Holy Spirit to give you sensitivity as you look over your day to be able to see the various ways God has been working in your life. The Spirit gives you freedom to look at your life in a way that is neither destructive nor condemnatory. Some feel this is a time to be really hard on yourself, when in fact it is an opportunity to see the ways you have responded to the gifts God has given to you during the day. Ask to learn and grow as you reflect on these issues, and in this manner you will deepen your knowledge of yourself and your relationship with God.

STEP THREE:
LOOK OVER YOUR DAY WITH GRATITUDE

Give thanks to the LORD, for he is good. "His love endures forever." (Psalm 136:1)

The third part of the prayer of examen focuses on giving thanks to God for all he has given to you during the day. Some will start from the moment they woke up and recall the events of their day by asking "What happened during the day?" The purpose of this question is to enable you to become an observer of your life. The following questions might help you.

- Was it a good or bad day?
- Did anything special happen today?
- Who were some of the people you encountered? What was this experience like?
- How did you feel about these experiences?

A key factor in this step is to become aware of your feelings as you process your day. If there is a deep sense of peace and consolation, you feel closer to God. On the other hand, if you are feeling distressed and upset, you need to explore the source of these feelings and how they might have moved you away from God. Taking all of this into consideration, begin to see how you can express gratitude to God.

STEP FOUR: REVIEW YOUR DAY

Examine yourselves to see whether you are living in the faith. Test yourselves. Do you not realize that Jesus Christ is in you? (2 Corinthians 13:5 NRSV)

This is the longest part of the prayer exercise. Recall the events of the day to see how you reacted. You may find at times that your heart is divided. This is not intended to focus on your failure, although there may be issues you need to address; rather, it is a time to see how you responded to God's gifts and opportunities. It is a time to see how you actively sought the presence of God in all you were doing and what difference this made in your life.

- Where did you love?
- Did you act freely toward others in a manner that was without an ulterior motive?
- Are there habits you have gotten into that seem to jump into place whenever you are in a typical situation? Do these help or hinder relationships?
- Where have you failed?

These simple questions help you become more focused on bringing Christ into every situation and circumstance of your life. You may find that you desire to change but do not seem to have the willpower to do so. This is what you offer to God, so that by the power of the Holy Spirit you will be changed into the person God desires you to be.

STEP FIVE: RECONCILE AND RESOLVE

"As the clay is in the potter's hand, so are you in my hand." (Jeremiah 18:6 NLT)

This final step in the prayer is an honest, transparent talk with the Lord.

You may be led to ask God for forgiveness or direction or simply to express gratitude for all God has done for you. If there are areas that need to be confessed, remember that God's desire is to allow you to experience healing grace and forgiveness. Be resolved to move forward in a different manner as you acknowledge that you are a recipient of God's grace and mercy.

EXERCISE

To offer the prayer of examen, use the following to help you voice your prayer.

1. **Today I am grateful for...**
   a.
   b.
   c.
   d.
   e.

2. **Today I saw God in my life when...**

3. **I felt disconnected to God when...**

4. **I need to accept that...**

5. **Tomorrow I want to...**

6. **My prayer to God is...**

---

[1] M. Scott Peck, *The Road Less Traveled: A New Psychology of Love, Traditional Values and Spiritual Growth* (New York: Touchstone Books, Simon & Schuster, 1978), 52.

"All things are shadows of the shining true:
Sun, sea, and air...
Every thing holds a slender guiding clue
Back to the mighty oneness."

—George MacDonald[1]

Section 2

FOUR

Scripture

PRAYERS

You are invited to use any of these prayers as a way of praying for yourself or for others. As you pray from Scripture, try to personalize what you are saying.

EPHESIANS 1:17–23

I keep asking that the God of our Lord Jesus Christ, the glorious Father, may give you the Spirit of wisdom and revelation, so that you may know him better. I pray also that the eyes of your heart may be enlightened in order that you may know the hope to which he has called you, the riches of his glorious inheritance in the saints, and his incomparably great power for us who believe. That power is like the working of his mighty strength, which he exerted in Christ when he raised him from the dead and seated him at his right hand in the heavenly realms, far above all rule and authority, power and dominion, and every title that can be given, not only in the present age but also in the one to come. And God placed all things under his feet and appointed him to be head over everything for the church, which is his body, the fullness of him who fills everything in every way.

EPHESIANS 3:16–21

I pray that out of his glorious riches he may strengthen you with power through his Spirit in your inner being, so that Christ may dwell in your hearts through faith. And I pray that you, being rooted and established in love, may have power, together with all the saints, to grasp how wide and long and high and deep is the love of Christ, and to know this love that surpasses knowledge—that you may be filled to the measure of all the fullness of God. Now to him who is able to do immeasurably more than all we ask or imagine, according to his power that is at work within us, to him be glory in the church and in Christ Jesus throughout all generations, for ever and ever! Amen.

PHILIPPIANS 1:3–6; 9–11

I thank my God every time I remember you. In all my prayers for all of you, I always pray with joy because of your partnership in the gospel from the first day until now, being confident of this, that he who began a good work in your will carry it on to completion until the day of Christ Jesus…And this is my prayer: that your love may abound more and more in knowledge and depth of insight, so that you may be able to discern what is best and may be pure and blameless until the day of Christ, filled with the fruit of righteousness that comes through Jesus Christ—to the glory and praise of God.

COLOSSIANS 1:9–14

We have not stopped praying for you and asking God to fill you with the knowledge of his will through all spiritual wisdom and understanding. And we pray this in order that you may live a life worthy of the Lord and may please him in every way: bearing fruit in every good work, growing in the knowledge of God, being strengthened with all power according to his glorious might so that you may have great endurance and patience, and joyfully giving thanks to the Father, who has qualified you to share in the inheritance of the saints in the kingdom of light. For he has rescued us from the dominion of darkness and brought us into the kingdom of the Son he loves, in whom we have redemption, the forgiveness of sins.

---

1 George MacDonald, *Diary of an Old Soul* (London: George Allen & Unwin Ltd., 1904), 96.

"My commonest attitude is this simple attentiveness, an habitual, loving, turning of my eyes to God."

—Brother Lawrence[1]

Section 3

PRAYING
the
PSALMS

Praying the psalms used to be a spiritual discipline that Christians did every day, either privately or corporately. Today, praying the psalms seems to be a forgotten spiritual discipline; in fact, it is uncommon that a psalm is read in its entirety in a worship service. However, the psalms are a great resource to enhance our prayers in that they reveal to us ways to express our grief, our deepest longings, our needs and our hurts, as well as our joy and our praise. As we pray the psalms we bring all aspects of our life before God. In doing this we learn how to share all of life with God and to trust God in all circumstances.

It is quite common to use the psalter as a prayer book, but to do so a couple of suggestions might be helpful. First, try to understand what the psalmist was writing about. What were the circumstances he was experiencing that caused him to write the particular psalm? How does his experience fit into your life at this moment? If the psalm does not resonate with your life at the present moment, consider how it addresses an issue in the lives of others you know.

Second, do not rush to read the psalm. Take time to meditate upon the words. See if there is a verse or a thought that seems to resonate with you. How might this lead you to pray for yourself or for others?

Some people pray the psalms sequentially; they begin at Psalm 1 and each day read the following one until they have completed all 150 psalms. Then they start the process all over. If you read a psalm in the morning and a psalm in the evening, you will read the entire psalter in two and a half months.

Do not worry about doing this perfectly; just begin. Allow the Holy Spirit to teach you and to guide you. Start slowly, and try this for about 20 minutes a day. After about three or four weeks, see if there is a difference in your life, in your relationship with God and in your relationships with others. The following list has placed the psalms in different categories that may help you if you are facing a particular situation.

TYPES OF PSALMS[2]

Thanksgiving and Praise

Psalm 57	God is glorious and loving.
Psalm 92	Pray and play on the Sabbath.
Psalm 95	To worship is to thank, praise, listen to and obey God.
Psalm 100	Thanksgiving leads to praise.
Psalm 107	Give thanks in times of consolation and desolation.
Psalm 136	Give thanks; God's love endures forever.
Psalm 103–107, 111–118, 134–139, 145–150	Sing hallelujah.

Wisdom

Psalm 1   You are blessed by delighting in God.

Psalm 4–5   Develop a rhythm of evening and morning prayer.

Psalm 8   Worship God the creator.

Psalm 19   Listen to God in creation.

Psalm 119   Delight in the law of God.

Confession and forgiveness

Psalm 32   Confess your sins, and you will be blessed.

Psalm 38   In your pain and guilt, cry out to God for help.

Psalm 51   Confess your sins to be restored and renewed.

Psalm 130   Wait for God's forgiveness.

Longing for God

Psalm 27   Seek God above all else.

Psalm 42   Long for God in the hard places.

Psalm 63   Desire God above all else.

Psalm 73   Make God the source of your strength.

Psalm 84   Desire the presence of God.

Comfort and Encouragement

Psalm 4   In your distress you can know God's love, joy and peace.

Psalm 16   Delight in God regardless of the circumstances of life.

Psalm 23   God is there to protect you.

Psalm 91   God protects, especially at night.

Psalm 121   The Lord protects on the journey of life.

Lament and Grief

Psalm 6   Pour out your tears to God.

Psalm 31   In times of distress, put your trust in God's presence.

Psalm 64   When verbally attacked, rely on God's justice.

Psalm 73   Praise and trust in God even when the wicked prosper.

Psalm 102   In desperation cry out to God and recall his care for you.

Psalm 142   Cry and complain to God and discover that he will meet your need.

Psalm 143   In trouble discover God's unfailing love.

Anger at Your Enemies

Psalm 35   When mistreated, let God fight for you.

Psalm 59   When slandered, trust God to defend you.

Psalm 69   When others hate you, express your anger to God.

Psalm 70   When others seek to harm you, cry out to God.

Psalm 109   When betrayed, vent your anger to God and rely on his love.

The Dark Night of the Soul
(Times When God Seems to Be Absent)

Psalm 13   When God's face is hidden, learn to trust him regardless.

Psalm 22   When it feels that God has rejected you, continue to praise him.

Psalm 77   When you don't feel God's love, meditate on his goodness.

Psalm 88   When you are in a deep pit and God seems angry, call out to him.

---

1 Brother Lawrence, *The Practice of the Presence of God,* trans. E. M. Blaiklock (Nashville: Thomas Nelson, 1981), 45.

2 Bill Gaultiere, "Praying the Psalms," available at http://www.soulshepherding.org/tag/praying-psalms/. Adapted and used with permission.

"The Word of Scripture should never stop sounding
in your ears and working in you all day long,
just like the words of someone you love.
And just as you do not analyze the words
of someone you love, but accept them as they are
said to you, accept the Word of Scripture and
ponder it in your heart, as Mary did.
That is all. That is meditation...Do not ask
'How shall I pass this on?' but
'What does it say to me?'
Then ponder this Word long in your heart
until it has gone right into you
and taken possession of you."

—Dietrich Bonhoeffer[1]

Section 4

The
PRACTICE
of
HOLY
READING

Many have learned to read the Bible for information; holy reading is a method of reading the Bible that helps you understand and hear God's Word in a way that can be transformational.[2] Through this approach you will discover an increasing ability to respond to what God has said as you offer yourself and your relationships to God.

THE PROCESS

There are four steps in the process of holy reading, beginning with Scripture and concluding with prayer.

Reading and Listening

The practice of holy reading requires that you develop the ability to hear what God is saying to you as you read the Scriptures. Find an inviting place where you will not be disturbed, and take a few moments to become still. Next, offer a prayer asking God to speak into your life from his Word. Read a short passage of Scripture, and as you are reading, listen for a word, phrase or concept that captures your attention. Some will find it helpful to read out loud, since this helps to slow down the pace, and it will keep your mind from wandering.

Meditation

Having read the text and listened for a word, phrase or concept that speaks to you in a personal manner, take a few minutes to meditate upon the section of text that you were drawn to. Meditation is more than thinking about an idea; to meditate means to ponder or to mull over in your mind a thought or concept. An example of meditation is found in Luke's Gospel when the shepherds came to Mary and Joseph and told them what the angel of the Lord had spoken: "Do not be afraid. I bring you good news of great joy that will be for all the people. Today in the town of David a Savior has been born to you: he is Christ the Lord" (Luke 2:10–11). Then we are told that Mary pondered all of this in her heart. In other words, she thought about what they said and the implications for her life, for her child and ultimately for the world. Meditation involves taking in the Word of God and allowing it to interact with your thoughts and hopes and dreams.

Prayer

God has spoken to us through the Bible, we have meditated upon what he has said, and now we speak back to God. This reinforces the concept that prayer is a dialogue and not a monologue. God speaks, and then you speak. Because God addresses different issues in each person's life, each of our prayers will be quite different. Your prayer might focus on thanking God for some insight he has given to you, or you might seek guidance from him, or you might ask God for forgiveness, or your prayer might be one of adoration and praise. Do not try to censor your prayer; that is, don't say what you think God wants to hear rather than speaking from your heart. Speak plainly and directly. What you will discover is that God's Word speaks powerfully into your life, and from that place you speak back to God.

Contemplation

The final movement of holy reading is to simply rest in the presence of God. There is no agenda. You have read God's Word and meditated upon it, and as God has spoken into your life, you have spoken back to God. Now you simply wait in his presence. For some this will be difficult, especially if you are an activist. If you find your mind wandering, simply go back and read the text, meditate on it and rest in the presence of God.

EXERCISE

If you are engaging in this practice for the first time, there are a few simple guidelines to follow that may be helpful.

1. **Listen to the Word of God.**

   Sit in silence for a few minutes.

   Read the passage slowly and possibly out loud.

   Listen for a word or idea that captures your attention.

   Say the word or idea over in your mind.

   Remain silent for two minutes following the reading as you meditate.

2. **Ask, how is my life touched by the Word of God?**

   Read the passage a second time.

   After reading the text, sit in silence for two minutes and meditate upon this question.

   Write down any insights that you might have received.

3. **Ask, what does God want me to do with this?**

   Read the passage a third time.

   After the reading, sit in silence for two minutes and meditate upon the question.

   Write down what you discern God wants you to do.

   Pray according to what God has spoken into your life. Some people find it helpful to write out the prayer. You can go back at a later date and reflect on what you have written.

4. **Rest in God.**

   When you conclude your prayer, simply rest in God's presence. As a reminder for later, you might write in your journal of how God has spoken to you through Scripture and your reflections on the process of holy reading.

   Conclude this time with a short prayer of thanksgiving.

SUGGESTED READINGS FOR A WEEK

- Day 1: Psalm 23
- Day 2: Isaiah 40:25–31
- Day 3: Matthew 6:25–34
- Day 4: John 13:1–17
- Day 5: Philippians 1:3–11
- Day 6: Colossians 1:9–14
- Day 7: Ephesians 1:15–21

---

[1] Dietrich Bonhoeffer, *The Way to Freedom: Letters, Lectures, and Notes, 1935–1939*, vol. 2 of *Collected Works of Dietrich Bonhoeffer*. ed. Edwin H. Robertson, trans. Edwin H. Robertson and John Bowden (London: Collins, 1996), 58–59.

[2] David Sherbino, *Re-Connect: Spiritual Exercises to Develop Intimacy with God* (Toronto: Castle Quay Books, 2013). Adapted and used with permission.

"The life of contemplation...is the life of the
Holy Spirit in our inmost soul.
The whole duty of contemplation
is to abandon what is base and trivial
in [your] life, and do all [you] can to conform...
to the secret and obscure promptings
of the Spirit of God.
This requires a constant discipline of humility,
obedience, self-distrust, prudence and above faith."

—Thomas Merton[1]

Section 5

The
PRACTICE
of
GOSPEL
CONTEMPLATION

Gospel contemplation is an approach to prayer that originated in the 8th century in an Italian monastery. John Veltri, S.J., explained that as the monks gathered for prayer and meditation one of the monks began to read from a passage of Scripture. After the first reading he paused for 30–40 seconds; then he read it again and paused at the end of the reading. This happened several times. After the final reading, the monks returned to their rooms and began to pray over the passage.

Through the process of repeated readings the monks became very familiar with the passage, and they began to see the gospel story as it unfolded. This approach enabled the monks to identify with a person in the story and even discover their inner feelings. Veltri states,

> The mystery of the gospel event would so take hold of the person at prayer that the past would become present through the instrument of imagination and memory. The memory of the person at prayer would be influenced by the memory of Jesus present now to the person praying.[2]

Ignatius of Loyola used gospel contemplation to describe this type of prayer whereby the readers entered the story through the gift of imagination with the purpose of allowing the story to reveal the Lord to them. Douglas Leonhardt states, "This prayer is not some kind of mystical prayer but a prayer form in which one uses his or her senses in an imaginative way to reflect on a Gospel passage."[3] Thus through this method the gospel story comes alive to the reader.

Veltri suggests that when you use gospel contemplation you are entering the life of Jesus through prayer. The following steps are offered by him as a way to do that.

First, select a short passage from the Gospels where Jesus is interacting with an individual.

Second, read the story over a couple of times so that the details are etched in your mind. Some find it helpful to read it aloud so that they grasp the emotion of the text. Between each reading remain in silence for about 30 seconds to allow the scene to sink into your imagination.

Third, reconstruct the story in your mind. It is helpful to ask the following questions: What is going on? How does Jesus interact with the various people? How do the people react to him? What emotions seem to be present?

Fourth, allow yourself to be part of the scene. Listen to what people are saying in the story. Look at what they are doing. As much as you can, try to take part in their activity; in this you are entering the story.

Fifth, as you reflect on the experience in prayer, share with the Lord what is happening to you through this particular encounter.

Sixth, after you have prayed, take a few moments to reflect on the whole experience and see if there is anything the Lord is directing you to return to at a later time.

SOME PASSAGES FOR REFLECTION

- The annunciation by the angel to Joseph (Matthew 1:18–25)
- The annunciation by the angel to Mary (Luke 1:26–38)
- The call of Levi (Mark 2:13–17)
- The faith of the Syrophoenician woman (Mark 7:24–30)
- The death of Lazarus (John 11:1–16)
- The washing of the disciples' feet (John 13:1–17)
- The reinstatement of Peter (John 21:15–19)

---

[1] Thomas Merton, quoted in Bruce Demarest, *Satisfy Your Soul: Restoring the Heart of Christian Spirituality* (Carol Stream: NavPress, 1999), 157.

[2] Adapted by John Veltri, S.J., from David Hassel, S.J., "Prayer of Christ's Memories," in *Sisters Today* (October 1977).

[3] Douglas J. Leonhardt, S.J., "Praying With Scripture," adapted from *Finding God in All Things: A Marquette Prayer Book* (Milwaukee: Marquette University Press, 2009), available at http://www.ignatianspirituality.com/ignatian-prayer/the-what-how-why-of-prayer/praying-with-scripture.

"Self-examination is not morbid introspection or self-condemnation, but the honest, fearless confrontation of the self, and its abandonment to God in trust."

—Kenneth Leech[1]

Section 6

Reflection

QUESTIONS

Many have never taken the time to look closely at their life and ask questions about some of the elementary issue that are fundamental to all of us. Yet these issues play a significant part in revealing who we are and how we live. Use the following questions as a guide to writing out your reflections.[2]

SELF-IMAGE

- What is your image of yourself?
- Are you an introverted person or an extroverted person?
- Are you a thinking person or a feeling person?
- What are the feelings you have about yourself?

YOUR VALUES

- What things are most important to you?
- What things do you desire most in life?
- How would you prioritize them?

- What determines the values you have listed?
- Who will benefit from your values? How?

YOUR COMMITMENTS

- What are your lifelong commitments?
- What are the commitments you presently have that are temporary?
- What are your commitments in life and in death?

YOUR RELATIONSHIPS

- Who are the significant people in your life at the present time?
- Describe these relationships.
- Who has been influential in your life? Explain.
- What are the difficult relationships in your life? Is there any way these can be changed or resolved?

YOUR VOCATION

- What do you consider to be God's calling on your life?
- In what way does your vocation bring honour and glory to God?
- What are your gifts? How are these gifts used in your vocation?
- What benefits do you receive from your vocation?
- What problems do you encounter in your vocation?
- If you could change one thing in your vocation, what would it be? How do you think you might do this? What keeps you from trying to make the change?

YOUR DREAMS

- Do you have a dream for your life?
- Are you in the process of fulfilling it?
- What are the challenges you face to fulfill your dream?
  Are there people who can help you to fulfill your dream?
- When your life is over, what would you like it to have
  meant?
- What words would you like to have inscribed on your
  tombstone as an epitaph?

---

1 Kenneth Leech, *True Prayer: An Invitation to Christian Spirituality* (San Francisco: Harper & Row, 1980, 1995).

2 Adapted from Ben Campbell Johnson, *To Will God's Will: Beginning the Journey* (Philadelphia: Westminster Press, 1987), 123.

"It is unlikely that we will deepen our relationship
with God in a casual or haphazard manner.
There will be a need for some intentional commitment
and some reorganization in our own lives."

—William Paulsell[1]

Section 7

The PRACTICE of DEVELOPING a Rule of LIFE

A rule of life sounds rather daunting for most. In fact, it may sound legalistic to impose rules to govern one's life. However, a rule of life is not intended to bring any form of bondage; rather, it is the means under God whereby we take responsibility for the pattern of our lives.

The rule of life was first established and made popular by St. Benedict, who sought to discern the will of God not only for himself but also for those who were a part of his community. Thus, a rule of life was designed as a guide to help people do the things they wanted and needed to do. Steve Macchia writes,

> *A rule of life helps us to clarify our deepest values, our most important relationships, our most authentic hopes and dreams, our most meaningful work, our highest priorities. It allows us to live with intention and purpose in the present moment.*[2]

A rule of life is holistic in that it helps us to examine different facets of life.

As you think about your life, explore the following topics:

RELATIONSHIPS

- What relationships do you have, and what roles do you play in them?
- In these various roles, what type of commitment is expected of you?
- Are there specific roles and relationships that God wants you to focus on during this season of your life?

TIME

- Think about how you spend time. This includes events that occur daily, weekly and monthly. There are some events that may happen only once a year.
- Do you take time to rest on a regular basis?
- Do you see a rhythm in your life that includes work and rest?
- Is there anything that is out of balance in how you spend your time?

CARING FOR THE BODY

- How would you describe your physical well-being?
- Do you regularly exercise?
- How do you relax?
- Do you have any outside interests?

The chart that follows is designed to help you think about what you are presently doing. Take some time to list all the activities and then bring this before God. By doing this activity you will begin to see that you already have a rule of life or patterns by which you live. See if there is balance in your life.

Prayerfully ask God if he is pleased with your present rule of life or if there are things that he may desire you to change. If God is prompting you to change, you may need to eliminate some things before you can add other things. God never stresses us out by placing demands on us that are not life-giving. You are encouraged to make incremental changes, as you will be able to see the difference they will make in your life. If you make too many changes at once you will likely fail, become discouraged and quit.

The accompanying chart enables you to consider four major areas of your life. First, look at your personal devotional spiritual life. Second, consider your involvement in your community as well as your faith community. Third, consider your involvement in family life, which changes according to the season of life you are in. Finally, look at the activities in your life, what are you doing in terms of work, rest, recreation and outside interests that are personally enriching.

Each category can be evaluated on a daily, weekly, monthly and yearly basis. The accompanying chart can be used to begin the process of establishing your personal rule of life.

TIME	PERSONAL DEVOTION	COMMUNITY	FAMILY	LIFE
Daily				
Weekly				
Monthly				
Yearly				

[1] William O. Paulsell, "Ways of Prayer: Designing a Personal Rule of Life," in *Weavings* 2, no. 5 (November–December 1987): 44.

[2] Stephen A. Macchia, *Crafting a Rule of Life* (Downers Grove: InterVarsity Press, 2012), 14.

"On earth we are wayfarers, always on the go.
This means that we have to keep on moving forward.
Therefore be always unhappy about where you
are if you want to reach where you are not.

If you are pleased with what you are,
you have stopped already.
If you say 'It is enough,' you are lost.
Keep on walking, moving forward,
trying for the goal."

—St. Augustine[1]

---

[1] St. Augustine, *Sermon* 169, 18.

CONTINUE
The
JOURNEY